Monumento a Lincoln

Julie Murray

Abdo
LUGARES SIMBÓLICOS
DE LOS ESTADOS UNIDOS
Kids

THIS BOOK CONTAINS
RECYCLED MATERIALS

Spanish Translator: Maria Puchol

Photo Credits: Getty Images, iStock, Library of Congress, Shutterstock,
©Rene Sturgell p.7 / CC-BY-SA-3.0, ©uplift_the_world p.11 / Shutterstock.com

Production Contributors: Teddy Borth, Jennie Forsberg, Grace Hansen

Design Contributors: Christina Doffing, Candice Keimig, Dorothy Toth

Publisher's Cataloging in Publication Data

Names: Murray, Julie, author.

Title: Monumento a Lincoln / by Julie Murray.

Other titles: Lincoln Memorial

Description: Minneapolis, Minnesota : Abdo Kids, 2018. | Series: Lugares
     simbólicos de los Estados Unidos | Includes bibliographical references and
     index.

Identifiers: LCCN 2016963075 | ISBN 9781532101878 (lib. bdg.) |
     ISBN 9781532102677 (ebook)

Subjects: LCSH: Lincoln Memorial (Washington, D.C.)--Juvenile literature. | Washington (D.C.)--
     Buildings, structures, etc.--Juvenile literature. | Spanish language materials--Juvenile literature.

Classification: DDC 975.3--dc23

LC record available at http://lccn.loc.gov/2016963075

Contenido

Monumento a Lincoln

Este **monumento homenajea** a Abraham Lincoln. Lincoln fue el presidente número 16 de Estados Unidos.

5

Nació en 1809 y vivió en una cabaña de madera.

Lo asesinaron de un disparo en 1865.

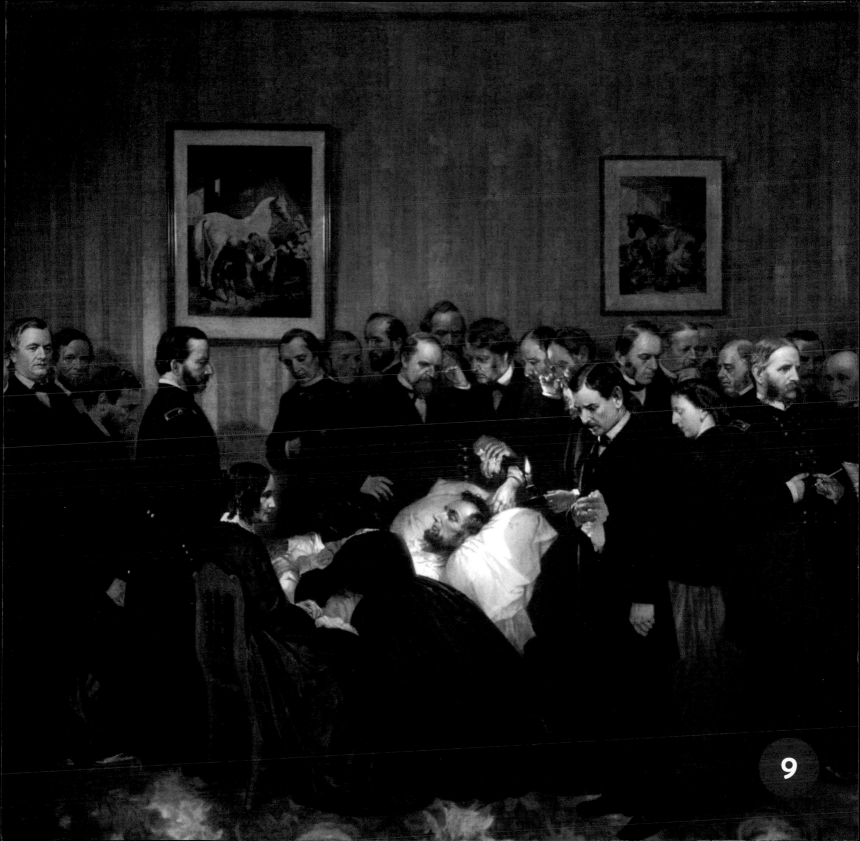

Le construyeron un **monumento**.

IN THIS TEMPLE
AS IN THE HEARTS OF THE PEOPLE
FOR WHOM HE SAVED THE UNION
THE MEMORY OF ABRAHAM LINCOLN
IS ENSHRINED FOREVER

QUIET
RESPECT
PLEASE

11

Está en Washington D.C.

13

Tardaron ocho años
en construirlo.

Hay una estatua de Lincoln dentro. Él está sentado en una silla.

QUIET
RESPECT
PLEASE

IN THIS TEMPLE
AS IN THE HEARTS OF THE PEOPLE
FOR WHOM HE SAVED THE UNION
THE MEMORY OF ABRAHAM LINCOLN
IS ENSHRINED FOREVER

17

En la pared están escritos

sus discursos.

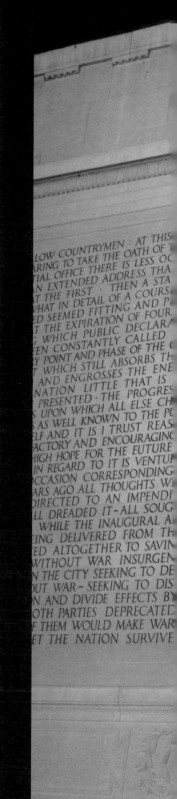

AND, THE OTHER WOULD ACCEPT WAR RATHER THAN LET IT PERISH · AND THE WAR CAME · ONE EIGHTH OF THE WHOLE POPULATION WERE COLORED SLAVES NOT DISTRIBUTED GENERAL- LY OVER THE UNION BUT LOCALIZED IN THE SOUTHERN PART OF IT · THESE SLAVES CONSTI- TUTED A PECULIAR AND POWERFUL INTEREST· ALL KNEW THAT THIS INTEREST WAS SOMEHOW THE CAUSE OF THE WAR · TO STRENGTHEN PER- PETUATE AND EXTEND THIS INTEREST WAS THE OBJECT FOR WHICH THE INSURGENTS WOULD REND THE UNION EVEN BY WAR WHILE THE GOV- ERNMENT CLAIMED NO RIGHT TO DO MORE THAN TO RESTRICT THE TERRITORIAL ENLARGE- MENT OF IT · NEITHER PARTY EXPECTED FOR THE WAR THE MAGNITUDE OR THE DURATION WHICH IT HAS ALREADY ATTAINED · NEITHER ANTICIPATED THAT THE CAUSE OF THE CONFLICT MIGHT CEASE WITH OR EVEN BEFORE THE CON- FLICT ITSELF SHOULD CEASE · EACH LOOKED FOR AN EASIER TRIUMPH AND A RESULT LESS FUN- DAMENTAL AND ASTOUNDING · BOTH READ THE SAME BIBLE AND PRAY TO THE SAME GOD AND EACH INVOKES HIS AID AGAINST THE OTHER· IT MAY SEEM STRANGE THAT ANY MEN SHOULD DARE TO ASK A JUST GOD'S ASSISTANCE IN WRINGING THEIR BREAD FROM THE SWEAT OF OTHER MEN'S FACES BUT LET US JUDGE NOT THAT WE BE NOT JUDGED · THE PRAYERS OF BOTH COULD NOT BE ANSWERED – THAT OF NEITHER HAS BEEN ANSWERED FULLY · THE ALMIGHTY HAS HIS OWN PURPOSES·"WOE UNTO THE WORLD BECAUSE OF OFFENSES FOR IT MUST NEEDS BE THAT OFFENSES COME BUT WOE TO THAT MAN BY WHOM THE OFFENSE COMETH·"

IF WE SHALL SUPPOSE THAT AMERICAN SLAVERY IS ONE OF THOSE OFFENSES WHICH IN THE PROVIDENCE OF GOD MUST NEEDS COME BUT WHICH HAVING CON- TINUED THROUGH HIS APPOINTED TIME HE NOW WILLS TO REMOVE AND THAT HE GIVES TO BOTH NORTH AND SOUTH THIS TERRIBLE WAR AS THE WOE DUE TO THOSE BY WHOM THE OFFENSE CAME SHALL WE DIS- CERN THEREIN ANY DEPARTURE FROM THOSE DIVINE ATTRIBUTES WHICH THE BELIEVERS IN A LIVING GOD ALWAYS ASCRIBE TO HIM · FONDLY DO WE HOPE – FERVENTLY DO WE PRAY – THAT THIS MIGHTY SCOURGE OF WAR MAY SPEEDILY PASS AWAY · YET IF GOD WILLS THAT IT CONTINUE UNTIL ALL THE WEALTH PILED BY THE BONDSMAN'S TWO HUNDRED AND FIFTY YEARS OF UN- REQUITED TOIL SHALL BE SUNK AND UNTIL EVERY DROP OF BLOOD DRAWN WITH THE LASH SHALL BE PAID BY ANOTHER DRAWN WITH THE SWORD AS WAS SAID THREE THOUSAND YEARS AGO SO STILL IT MUST BE SAID "THE JUDGMENTS OF THE LORD ARE TRUE AND RIGHTEOUS ALTOGETHER·"

WITH MALICE TOWARD NONE WITH CHARITY FOR ALL WITH FIRMNESS IN THE RIGHT AS GOD GIVES US TO SEE THE RIGHT LET US STRIVE ON TO FINISH THE WORK WE ARE IN TO BIND UP THE NATION'S WOUNDS TO CARE FOR HIM WHO SHALL HAVE BORNE THE BAT- TLE AND FOR HIS WIDOW AND HIS ORPHAN- TO DO ALL WHICH MAY ACHIEVE AND CHER- ISH A JUST AND LASTING PEACE AMONG OURSELVES AND WITH ALL NATIONS ·

Mucha gente lo visita cada año.

MICHIGAN FLORIDA TEXAS IOWA WISCONSIN CALIFORNIA MINNESOTA OREGON KANSAS WEST VIRGINIA NEVADA NEBRASKA COLORADO NORTH DAKOTA

Más datos

Hay 36 columnas
a su alrededor

El discurso de Gettysburg
está grabado en la pared

Mide 99 pies de
altura (30 m)

La estatua está hecha
de mármol

Glosario

homenajear
mostrar gran respeto y admiración hacia alguien.

monumento
construcción que se hace para recordar a una persona o evento.

Índice

abdokids.com

¡Usa este código para entrar en abdokids.com y tener acceso a juegos, arte, videos y mucho más!

Código Abdo Kids:
ULK9114